THE INSTITUTIONAL CODE OF FOREX

14 STEPS TO READ THE MARKETS LIKE A BANK

SwipeUP
Elite FX Method

ANDREA RUSSO

ANDREA RUSSO

The Institutional Code of Forex

14 Steps to Read the Markets Like a Bank - SwipeUP Elite FX Method

First published by Andrea Russo 2025

First edition

This book was professionally typeset on Reedsy.
Find out more at reedsy.com

Contents

Introduction

Imagine the Forex market as a vast ocean. Millions of traders navigate it every day, but only a few—very few—truly manage to make a consistent profit. The truth is simple: most lose because they don't understand who really moves the market.

Behind every candlestick that lights up on the chart, there's no magic, but the decisions of institutions: central banks, investment funds, hedge funds. They don't "follow" the price: they create it. And they do so with a specific goal: to push the mass of retail traders (i.e., small investors) in the wrong direction, then collect the liquidity they leave behind.

The SwipeUP Elite FX Method was created precisely for this:

to read the market through the eyes of
institutions;
to understand what they're really doing behind the scenes;
to act against the crowd, not with it.
What does it mean to "invest like a bank"?

Banks don't buy or sell by intuition. They analyze hundreds of data points: volumes, positioning, options, monetary policy, macroeconomic events, and correlated movements between currencies. Only when everything is aligned do they enter a position.

SwipeUP Elite FX replicates this logic in an accessible version. Each decision passes through 14 analysis steps, each dedicated to a specific aspect of the market (technical, statistical, institutional, psychological, macroeconomic). It's like a giant engine that filters the data and tells you whether the trade is truly "institutional" or a retail trap.

Why you need a method before investing

In Forex, the winner isn't the one who's "right" about the price, but the one who knows how to wait for the right moment. 90% of traders lose because they enter too early, without knowing:

where others are positioned;
what the banks are doing;
what news is about to be released;
if the volatility is sufficient;
if the trade actually makes statistical sense.

SwipeUP Elite FX helps block all imperfect trades. As long as even one module gives an inconsistent signal, you don't enter. Only when all 14 steps confirm together is the trade ready: it's as if the market were saying "now it's your turn."

How it works in practice

Each analysis starts from the actual entry point, with Stop Loss and Take Profit already defined. From there, the method:

collects data from at least three real, independent sources for each critical parameter;

simulates 10 possible scenarios, verifying in which case the price touches the TP or SL first;

eliminates the trade if even one realistic scenario results in a loss before the profit;

performs stress tests, backtests, and candlestick predictions with up to 95% reliability;

calculates the Confidence Score: only above 70/100 is the trade valid.

Institutional Mindset

SwipeUP Elite FX is not just analysis, it's also discipline. Emotions are the trader's greatest enemy. This is why the method includes emotional risk rules:

two consecutive stops → stop;

excessive drawdown → recalculate;

trade too close to "killer" times → don't enter.

"I execute the plan, I don't suffer it. I operate like the institutions, against the retail market. Discipline and patience above all."

Before you begin

Before even opening a trade, a novice must:

understand that the market is not random, but intelligently manipulated;

accept that the method is the compass, not instinct;

know that each trade must be built with real data, not opinions;

train patience: sometimes the best trade is to do nothing.

Only in this way can the trader stop being part of the crowd and begin to think like someone who truly moves the market.

1

First Step – Multi-Timeframe Technical Analysis

Understanding the Bigger Picture Before You Trade

Before you place a single trade in the Forex market,
you must learn one essential truth:
☞ **There isn't just one market — there are many, layered inside each other.**
Each *timeframe* (the period represented by a single candle) shows a different part of the same story.
Looking at only one is like starting a movie from minute 47 — you might guess what's happening, but you'll never know *why*.

🎯 Goal of This Step

To understand where the current price is located inside the larger market structure.
You'll learn to recognize whether you're trading:

- within the **main trend** (the dominant, long-term move),
- inside a **temporary correction**, or
- within a **phase of accumulation or distribution**
- (when institutions prepare the next big move).

Only after identifying your exact position in this cycle can you find the right moment to enter.

🔍 What Multi-Timeframe Analysis Means

The SwipeUP Elite FX Method always works **top-down**, from the largest timeframe to the smallest:

1. **Monthly (MN):** shows the institutional, long-term direction — where central banks are steering.
2. **Weekly (W1):** defines the dominant trend and key zones of support/resistance.
3. **Daily (D1):** identifies the medium-term structure and market rhythm.
4. **8-Hour (H8):** the main operational timeframe of SwipeUP Elite FX.
5. **1-Hour (H1) and 15-Minute (M15):** used *only* for precise entries — never for choosing direction.

Each level must align with the one above it.
If even one shows an opposite signal, the trade is blocked: it means the market isn't yet synchronized.

📈 How to Read Market Structure

Price always moves in two alternating phases:
impulses and **corrections.**

- An **impulse** is a strong move in the main direction.
- A **correction** is a temporary pullback that reloads liquidity
- for the next institutional push.

On the chart, this appears as a sequence of highs and lows.
Your job is to recognize whether the current move is a:

- **continuation** (joining the trend), or
- **reversal** (beginning of an opposite move).

👉 **Example:**
If the D1 chart shows lower highs and lower lows (downtrend), but the H1 chart rises sharply, that's not a reversal — it's a correction.
Banks are simply reloading short positions higher.

🧠 How Institutions Think

Institutions operate across multiple horizons at once:
they *build* positions on monthly and weekly charts
but *execute* them on lower ones (8H, 4H, 1H).
Movements that look "random" to a retail trader
are actually the sum of thousands of coordinated micro-trades
executed across timeframes.
That's why SwipeUP Elite FX follows a logical sequence:

1. Identify the main structure on MN and W1.
2. Find institutional zones on D1 (where banks entered before).
3. Confirm directional coherence on H8.
4. Look for the entry pattern on H1/M15.

✅ Only when *all* levels align is Step 1 complete.

⚠️ Common Beginner Mistakes

- Entering a trend just because "it looks like it's going up."
- Watching only one timeframe (usually M15 or H1).
- Failing to notice when a trend has already exhausted.
- Ignoring the weekly or monthly context.

These mistakes lead traders to buy when institutions are selling.

Connection to the Next Steps

Step 1 is the foundation on which everything else stands. Without a proper multi-timeframe view:

- **Price Action (Step 2)** loses meaning,
- **Support/Resistance (Step 3)** becomes unreliable, and
- **Pattern Statistics (Step 9)** become distorted.

Only after seeing the full picture can you analyze the smaller details.

"Before you act, observe from above.
The market is like a river --
only from the sky can you see where it flows."

2

Step 2 – Price Action Learning the Language of Price

If the trend is the direction of the river,
then **Price Action** is the current that reveals its strength.
Many traders depend on indicators or automated signals,
but the truth is simple:
price alone already contains all the information you need.
Each candle tells a story —
who won between buyers and sellers,
where institutions have accumulated orders,
and where retail traders are about to be trapped.
Price Action is the market's native language.
Once you learn to read it,
you can anticipate institutional moves
and spot the exact points where the trend truly shifts.

🎯 Goal of This Step

To train your eyes to read the chart
the way a **bank analyst** would:
Understanding why a candle forms the way it does,
what each sequence of highs and lows represents,
and when a movement is real versus when it's a trap.
In short — to recognize **institutional behavior hidden inside every candle.**

🔍 What Price Action Really Means

Price Action means studying the raw movement of price
without relying on external indicators.
Each candle gives you four key data points:

- **Open** – where the battle begins
- **High** – the highest point buyers reached
- **Low** – the deepest point sellers reached
- **Close** – where the fight ended

Together, these reveal the internal structure of the market.
The candle's *color* (green or red) is just the final chapter of that story.
In SwipeUP Elite FX, Price Action is used to determine whether the current movement is:

- an **impulse** (a genuine institutional move), or
- a **correction** (a pause before the next push).

Practical Example

Imagine price rising quickly for several hours.
A beginner might think:

> *"It's going up! I should buy."*

But an institutional trader knows better —
that rise could simply be a **liquidity trap**,
designed to lure retail traders in before a reversal.
When banks want to sell big volumes,
they need buyers.
So first they *push* the price higher to create them.
Once the crowd buys, the institutions sell —
and the market reverses violently.

How to Recognize It

- Candles with **long wicks on top** and closes near the bottom →
- buyers trapped, institutions selling.
- Candles with **strong full bodies and high closes** →
- true institutional buying.

How Institutions Think

Banks never enter with one click.
They build liquidity first.
If they plan to buy millions of euros,
they first drive price lower —
so that retail traders panic and start selling.

Only then, when enough liquidity is available,
they buy everything back.
You'll see a big red candle —
and right after, the market explodes upward.
It's not random: it's strategy.

> 🧠 Retail traders see danger;
> institutions see opportunity.

How to Apply Price Action Step by Step

1. **Observe D1 and H8 charts.**
2. These show the main structure and institutional footprint.
3. **Mark liquidity zones.**
4. Areas with long wicks or repeated rejections.
5. → These are where retail stop losses accumulate.
6. **Identify manipulation.**
7. If price breaks a level then quickly reverses,
8. that was a **liquidity grab.**
9. **Wait for confirmation.**
10. Once a strong candle closes in the opposite direction,
11. the real institutional move begins.
12. → This is where SwipeUP looks for *entry post-manipulation.*

📊 Key Visual Patterns

Candle Signal Meaning Institutional Interpretation

Long upper wick

Rejection of selling zone

Banks selling above that level

Long lower wick

Liquidity collection
Banks buying at discount
Small, sideways candles
Accumulation phase
Volatility building up
Large, full-body candle
Institutional impulse
Real directional move
Price Action is a **visual language** —
the more you observe it,
the more fluent you become.

⚠️ Common Beginner Mistakes

1. **Seeing patterns everywhere.**
2. Not every pin bar or engulfing means a trade.
3. Context matters — only trust signals in institutional zones.
4. **Using only small timeframes.**
5. M15 and H1 are noise;
6. true institutional footprints live on D1 and H8.
7. **Ignoring the bigger picture.**
8. A strong candle against the main trend is usually just a trap.
9. **Acting on impulse.**
10. Price is not an invitation — it's information.
11. Learn to interpret before reacting.

💪 What This Step Changes for You

Once you understand Price Action,
the chart stops looking chaotic.
Every candle has meaning.

You'll see where liquidity hides,
where manipulation happens,
and where the real move begins.

> 📊 Price doesn't lie —
> it whispers the truth to those who know its language.

Connection with the Other Steps

- Step 1 taught you *where* you are in the market.
- Step 2 teaches you *how* price behaves inside that structure.
- Step 3 will show you *where* price stops, pauses, and turns —
- through support and resistance levels.

Together, these three steps form
the technical foundation of the SwipeUP Elite FX Method.

```
"Price always speaks.
 Only those who listen carefully
 can hear when the banks are entering."
```

3

Step 3 – Support and Resistance Finding the Points Where the Market Stops and Turns

In every market, price moves like a wave —
surging forward, pausing, and then retreating.
But have you ever noticed that it often stops
around the same price levels again and again?
Those are not coincidences.
They are **Support and Resistance zones** —
the invisible walls where banks, hedge funds, and market makers
have placed their biggest orders.
The **Third Step of the SwipeUP Elite FX Method**
teaches you to recognize these zones,
to understand *why* price stops there,
and to use them as your navigation map inside the market.

🎯 Goal of This Step

To identify the price areas
where institutions are most active —
the levels where liquidity accumulates,
orders are triggered, and new trends begin.
Once you learn to see these zones clearly,
you stop chasing price
and start waiting where the market must return.

> 💡 Smart traders don't chase the wave —
> they wait where it always comes back.

🔍 What Are Support and Resistance

- **Support**: a price area where buyers (demand) enter the market,
- stopping or reversing a downtrend.
- **Resistance**: a price area where sellers (supply) appear,
- halting or reversing an uptrend.

They are not single lines, but *zones*
created by clusters of institutional orders.
The market remembers these zones —
because the institutions that moved price there once
often defend or attack them again later.

📈 How to Draw Support and Resistance Correctly

1. **Use the Daily (D1) and 8-Hour (H8) charts first.**
2. These show the zones that truly matter to institutions.
3. **Mark the areas where price reversed multiple times.**
4. If price touches a level 2–3 times and rejects it strongly,
5. that's a valid zone.
6. **Treat them as *ranges*, not thin lines.**
7. Support and Resistance often span 20–50 pips depending on volatility.
8. **Look for "liquidity shadows."**
9. Long wicks that pierce the zone and return inside it
10. usually signal stop hunts — proof of institutional activity.

🧠 How Institutions Use These Levels

Institutions don't respect your lines — they *create* them.
They know that retail traders place their stop losses
just above resistance or below support.
So, what do they do?
They **push price beyond those levels**
to trigger retail stops, collect liquidity,
and then reverse the market in the opposite direction.
This is called a **false breakout** or **liquidity grab**.

> 🧠 The level you fear most
> is often where banks enter with size.

⚙️ How SwipeUP Elite FX Analyzes These Zones

Each Support and Resistance zone is validated by three filters:

Filter What It Checks Why It Matters

Volume & OI Confirmation

Rising volume near the level

Confirms institutional orders present

Sentiment Divergence

Retail buying at resistance or selling at support

Classic trap setup

Price Action Reaction

Strong wick or engulfing candle from the zone

Confirms liquidity absorption

If all three align → zone is **institutionally valid**.

If even one fails → zone ignored.

📊 Example

On **EUR/USD**, price falls sharply to 1.0700, touches it three times, and bounces each time. At the same time:

- Volume increases at that level,
- Retail traders are mostly short (70%),
- A strong bullish engulfing candle appears.

Result → **Institutional Support Zone confirmed.** Banks likely accumulating buy positions. The next move? A breakout above the last swing high — fueled by trapped shorts.

How to Trade Around These Zones

1. **Mark institutional zones on D1 and H8.**
2. These are your *battlefields.*
3. **Wait for a manipulation (fake break).**
4. The spike beyond the level creates liquidity.
5. **Enter only after confirmation.**
6. Once a candle closes back inside the zone,
7. the real direction begins.
8. **Set your Stop Loss beyond the manipulation wick.**
9. It protects your position from another sweep.
10. **Aim your Take Profit at the next opposite zone.**

⚠️ Common Mistakes

1. **Using single lines instead of zones.**
2. The market breathes — levels are areas, not millimeters.
3. **Drawing too many levels.**
4. Focus only on the strongest 3–4 per timeframe.
5. **Entering before confirmation.**
6. Patience is your most profitable indicator.
7. **Ignoring volume and sentiment.**
8. Without these, your level is just a guess.

💪 What This Step Teaches You

Once you master Support and Resistance,
you stop reacting — you start *anticipating.*
You'll know where the market is likely to pause,
where retail traders will fall into traps,
and where the institutions are quietly waiting.

📊 Support and Resistance are not barriers —
they're launchpads for institutional orders.

Connection with the Other Steps

- **Step 1** gave you the market's overall structure.
- **Step 2** taught you to read each candle.
- **Step 3** now anchors your vision —
- showing where those candles truly matter.

From here, Step 4 will reveal
how to recognize *breakouts* and *retests* that follow these key zones.

```
"The market always returns to where the big money is waiting.
 Find those places -- and you'll never chase price again."
```

4

Step 4 - Breakout and Retest Learning to Trade the Moment the Market Reveals Its True Direction

Every chart tells a story of tension.
Price moves between zones of support and resistance,
bouncing like a ball inside a box —
until the moment when pressure builds so much
that it finally **breaks out**.
That instant is what traders call a **Breakout**.
But not every breakout is real.
Some are pure deception — traps set by institutions
to lure retail traders in before reversing.
The **Fourth Step of the SwipeUP Elite FX Method**
teaches you how to tell the difference between a real breakout
and a false one,
and how to use the **retest** to enter with the same precision as

the banks.

🎯 Goal of This Step

To recognize when a market is ready to explode beyond a key zone,
and to wait for the confirmation that makes the move *safe* and *institutional*.
The goal isn't to chase the breakout itself,
but to master **the retest** —
the moment when the market returns to test the level it just broke.

> 💡 Retail traders trade the breakout.
> Professionals trade the retest.

🔍 What Is a Breakout

A **breakout** happens when price finally escapes
a clear zone of support or resistance
after multiple failed attempts.
It's the market's way of declaring:

> *"A new phase has begun."*

But here's the catch —
many breakouts are **false**, created intentionally
to trigger stop losses and fill institutional orders.
That's why SwipeUP Elite FX never trades the first spike.
It waits for the *retest* to confirm
that the breakout is backed by real institutional liquidity.

📈 How to Identify a Real Breakout

1. **Volume Confirmation**
2. → Real breakouts occur on rising institutional volume.
3. → False ones happen in silence.
4. **Clean Structure**
5. → Before breaking, the market compresses —
6. smaller candles, decreasing volatility.
7. → Then one strong candle expands through the zone.
8. **Close Outside the Zone**
9. → The candle body must close clearly beyond the level,
10. not just wick through it.
11. **Retest Reaction**
12. → After the breakout, price returns to the level.
13. If it holds, the breakout is confirmed.
14. If it breaks back inside, it was a fake.

🧠 How Institutions Use Breakouts

Banks know exactly where retail traders place orders.
When price breaks above resistance,
thousands of retail buy orders trigger at once.
What do the banks do?
They sell into those orders —
collecting liquidity and reversing the move.
A few hours later, the price falls back below the breakout level.
Retail traders are trapped,
and institutions are now on the winning side.
The SwipeUP Elite FX Method waits for that retest moment —
the point where banks quietly reenter
while the crowd is still confused.

🧠 Institutions create the breakout to find liquidity.
The real move begins when everyone thinks it's over.

⚙️ How to Trade the Retest with SwipeUP Elite FX

1. **Identify the Breakout Zone (from Step 3).**
2. Mark the area of support/resistance clearly on H8 or D1.
3. **Wait for a Strong Breakout Candle.**
4. It must close *fully* outside the zone, not just touch it.
5. **Watch the Retest.**
6. Price often returns to the level within 1–3 candles.
7. **Look for Price Action Confirmation.**

- Bullish engulfing candle after a breakout up
- Bearish engulfing candle after a breakout down

1. **Enter with Institutional Logic.**

- Entry: at the retest confirmation candle
- Stop Loss: just beyond the opposite side of the zone
- Take Profit: next major institutional level

📊 Example

On **GBP/USD**,
price breaks above resistance at 1.2700 with a strong candle.
Retail traders rush to buy immediately.
Then price pulls back to 1.2700 — the *retest*.
At that point, volume spikes again,
and a bullish engulfing candle forms.

That's where the SwipeUP trader enters.
Price continues to 1.2860 —
a clean institutional move while the retail crowd exits in confusion.

⚠️ Common Mistakes

1. **Chasing the breakout candle.**
2. The market will often reverse right after you enter.
3. **Ignoring volume.**
4. No volume = no real breakout.
5. **Trading inside the zone.**
6. Wait until price *leaves* the box and confirms it.
7. **Forgetting the retest.**
8. Patience is what separates a lucky trade from a professional one.

💪 What This Step Teaches You

Once you master Breakouts and Retests,
you'll stop reacting to fake moves.
You'll understand that markets don't explode randomly —
they build pressure, test, and release in perfect rhythm.
The breakout is just the spark.
The retest is where the institutions load the fire.

📊 Retail traders see a line breaking.
Institutions see a door opening.

Connection with the Other Steps

- **Step 3** gave you the map — the zones where pressure builds.
- **Step 4** shows you *when* and *how* that pressure releases.
- The next steps will teach you to use indicators
- and statistics to confirm these breakout movements
- with precision and confidence.

```
"Don't rush through the open door.
 Wait until the market walks back and holds it open
 for you."
```

5

Step 5 – Technical Indicators Turning Numbers into Clarity

Charts can be overwhelming at first —
lines, colors, candles everywhere.
That's where **technical indicators** come in.
Indicators are not magic formulas;
they are **tools for reading market behavior more clearly**.
They help you see what price is already showing —
but in a more structured and measurable way.
The **Fifth Step of the SwipeUP Elite FX Method**
teaches you how to use indicators as confirmation,
not as decision-makers.
Because in the institutional world,
indicators never lead — they follow.

🎯 Goal of This Step

To understand how to use the right indicators
to **support** your analysis — not replace it.
Indicators in SwipeUP Elite FX are filters:
they confirm what the multi-timeframe structure (Step 1),
Price Action (Step 2),
and Support/Resistance (Step 3) have already suggested.

> 💡 The indicator doesn't predict the market —
> it measures how aligned the market already is.

🔍 What Are Technical Indicators

A **technical indicator** is a mathematical formula
applied to price or volume data
to make hidden information visible.
They can show:

- Momentum (how strong a move is),
- Trend direction (where it's heading),
- Volatility (how fast it's moving),
- or Volume activity (who's behind it).

The key is to understand **what each one truly tells you** —
and when to ignore it.

📊 The Core Indicators in SwipeUP Elite FX

1. Moving Averages (MA, EMA, SMA)

They smooth out price action to reveal the trend.

- If price stays above the 200-period MA → long-term up-trend.
- If it's below → long-term downtrend.
- The slope (angle) of the MA shows momentum.
- A flat MA means consolidation.

2. WaveTrend Oscillator (WT1 & WT2)

Used to detect institutional momentum and reversals.

- When both lines cross up from oversold → accumulation phase.
- When both cross down from overbought → distribution phase.
- The SwipeUP Elite FX system uses this as a *timing filter*
- for entries aligned with higher-timeframe trends.

3. Relative Strength Index (RSI)

Measures speed and intensity of movements.

- Above 70 → strong momentum or exhaustion.
- Below 30 → potential accumulation.
- Institutions often use RSI to trap retail traders —
- what looks "overbought" can stay that way for weeks in real trends.

4. Average True Range (ATR)

Shows market volatility.
It's vital for risk management:

- A larger ATR = wider stops and targets.
- A smaller ATR = tighter trades.
- SwipeUP uses ATR to set logical Stop Loss and Take Profit distances.

🧠 How Institutions View Indicators

Institutions don't trade based on indicator signals.
They use them to **measure liquidity, volatility, and crowd behavior**.
When retail traders all buy because the RSI crosses 70, institutions see that as a signal of **liquidity concentration** — perfect to sell into.
SwipeUP Elite FX inverts that logic:
we use indicators to see *what the crowd sees* —
so we can do the opposite.

> 🧠 The crowd uses indicators to decide.
> Institutions use them to predict the crowd.

⚙️ How to Use Indicators Correctly

1. **Start from structure, not from signals.**
2. Never open a trade just because an indicator changes color
3. **Use confluence.**
4. Wait for 2–3 indicators to confirm

5. what your technical analysis already suggests.
6. **Match indicators to timeframe.**

- D1/H8 → trend indicators (MA, RSI)
- H1/M15 → timing indicators (WT, stochastic)

1. **Avoid indicator overload.**
2. More charts ≠ more precision.
3. Keep only what helps you make decisions faster.

📈 Example

You're analyzing **AUD/CHF**:

- Price is below the 200 MA → long-term downtrend.
- WaveTrend crosses down from the overbought zone on H8.
- RSI is near 60 and turning lower.

Result → all indicators confirm institutional bearish pressure.
SwipeUP marks this as a valid setup only if
Price Action (Step 2) also supports it with a manipulation pattern.
Indicators confirm — they don't decide.

⚠️ Common Mistakes

1. **Trading every crossover.**
2. Markets breathe; not every signal means a new trend.
3. **Mixing incompatible indicators.**
4. For example, RSI and Stochastic both measure momentum — redundant.

5. **Ignoring the higher timeframe.**
6. An H1 buy signal inside a D1 downtrend = trap.
7. **Believing indicators can predict.**
8. They summarize past data — they don't foresee the future.

💪 What This Step Teaches You

After mastering indicators,
you'll stop using them as a crutch
and start treating them as precision tools.
You'll know which ones truly matter,
how to align them with the bigger market picture,
and when to ignore them completely.

> 📊 Indicators don't lead the price —
> they confirm the truth already written in it.

Connection with the Other Steps

- **Step 4** showed you *when* price breaks structure.
- **Step 5** now helps you *measure* that movement.
- The next step, Step 6, will take you deeper
- into harmonic and cyclical patterns —
- the rhythm that ties all market movements together.

"Indicators are like instruments in an airplane.
You don't stare at them all the time --
you glance at them to stay on course."

6

Step 6 – Harmonic and Cyclical Patterns Discovering the Hidden Rhythm of the Market

If price were a song,
harmonic and cyclical patterns would be its rhythm.
While most traders see chaos on the chart,
institutions know that markets move
in **recurring mathematical structures** —
patterns that repeat because human behavior repeats.
The **Sixth Step of the SwipeUP Elite FX Method**
teaches you to recognize these invisible geometries,
to spot where the market is in its natural cycle,
and to use that knowledge to anticipate reversals
long before they become obvious.

🎯 Goal of This Step

To identify **recurring patterns and cycles** that reveal when a movement is likely to end and a new one is about to begin.
This allows you to enter trades with precise timing, aligned with both **technical logic** and **market psychology**.

> 💡 The market doesn't repeat perfectly — but it always rhymes.

🔍 What Are Harmonic and Cyclical Patterns

Harmonic Patterns

These are geometric formations based on Fibonacci ratios.

They represent price symmetry — the balance between impulse and correction.

The most common harmonic patterns used in SwipeUP Elite FX are:

- **Gartley (AB=CD)**
- **Bat**
- **Butterfly**
- **Crab**
- **Cypher**

Each pattern is built on Fibonacci retracements and extensions (0.382, 0.618, 1.27, 1.618...) that show where price is likely to turn.

Cyclical Patterns

These are **time-based patterns** —
repetitions in how long impulses and corrections last.
For example:

- After every strong 3–5 day rally,
- markets often correct for 1–2 days.
- Major weekly cycles tend to repeat every 30–45 days.

Institutions track these cycles
because capital flows move rhythmically through the global economy.

📈 Example of a Harmonic Pattern

Imagine EUR/USD forming this sequence:

- XA: price rises 300 pips
- AB: retraces 61.8%
- BC: extends 38.2%
- CD: completes 127.2% of XA

This forms a **Bullish Gartley Pattern**.
At point D, institutional algorithms detect geometric confluence,
and liquidity starts shifting —
buyers begin accumulating while retail traders are still shorting.
SwipeUP identifies that completion point as a **potential reversal zone (PRZ)**,

confirming it only if sentiment, volume, and Price Action agree.

🧠 How Institutions Use Patterns

Institutional trading desks don't use harmonic names like "Gartley" —
but their algorithms are built around the same logic:
price symmetry, volatility expansion, and time cycles.
They accumulate positions quietly inside those zones,
using pattern-based liquidity as cover.
Retail traders, unaware of these cycles,
believe the trend continues —
while institutions are already preparing the next phase.

> 🧠 Institutions don't follow patterns —
> they create the conditions for them to repeat.

⚙️ How to Apply Harmonic and Cyclical Analysis

1. **Identify the Pattern**

- Look for symmetrical movements (AB=CD) on D1 or H8 charts.
- Use Fibonacci retracement tools to measure ratios.

1. **Confirm with Other Steps**

- Step 1: Multi-timeframe direction must align.
- Step 5: Indicators should confirm momentum exhaustion.
- Step 14 (later): Relative currency strength must support

reversal logic.

1. **Mark the Potential Reversal Zone (PRZ)**

- Combine Fibonacci levels and previous institutional zones (from Step 3).

1. **Wait for Price Action Confirmation**

- Bullish or bearish engulfing candles.
- Volume spike or sentiment shift.

1. **Set Entry and Exit**

- Entry: after confirmation candle.
- Stop Loss: just beyond point X.
- Take Profit: at next Fibonacci target (0.618 or 1.0 projection).

📊 Example of a Cyclical Pattern

On GBP/JPY, you notice that every rally lasts 4–5 days,
followed by a 2-day correction.
You mark this as a **short-term cycle**.
When the next 4-day rally completes
and sentiment turns extreme,
you prepare for a correction trade.
SwipeUP confirms with momentum indicators and sentiment divergence —
a high-probability setup forms exactly when the cycle resets.

⚠️ Common Mistakes

1. **Forcing patterns that don't fit.**
2. Not every zigzag is a harmonic pattern.
3. **Ignoring confluence.**
4. A pattern alone means nothing without volume, sentiment, or structure alignment.
5. **Using only one timeframe.**
6. Patterns must align across multiple timeframes.
7. **Expecting perfect geometry.**
8. Real markets are fluid; accept small deviations.

💪 What This Step Teaches You

Once you learn to see harmonics and cycles,
you stop being surprised by reversals.
You'll recognize when the market is simply completing its rhythm
and when a new movement is forming.
Trading becomes less about guessing
and more about understanding the music behind the price.

> 📊 The market is not random —
> it dances to a rhythm you can learn to hear.

Connection with the Other Steps

- **Step 5** gave you quantitative tools (indicators).
- **Step 6** adds the element of *time and geometry*.
- In the next step, you'll study **volume and market profile** —
- how institutional orders shape those patterns from within.

```
"When you understand the rhythm of the market,
 you stop chasing noise
 and start trading music."
```

7

Step 7 – Volume and Market Profile Analysis Seeing What the Banks See

Imagine walking into a room full of traders —
everyone shouting, buying, selling, reacting to every tick.
You can't hear all the words,
but if you could *measure the volume of their voices*,
you'd know who's really in control.
That's what **volume analysis** does.
It lets you see the footprints of the institutions —
where they're entering, where they're exiting,
and where they've left their money behind.
The **Seventh Step of the SwipeUP Elite FX Method**
teaches you how to read that hidden layer of information:
the energy behind every move.

🎯 Goal of This Step

To learn how to identify **where institutional money is active**, so you can follow the real flow of capital instead of reacting to price alone. While retail traders look at candles, professional traders look at *volumes and clusters.*

> 💡 Price shows what happened.
> Volume shows who made it happen.

🔍 What Is Volume and Market Profile

Volume

Represents how many contracts, lots, or orders were traded during a specific period. High volume = institutional interest. Low volume = retail noise or indecision.

Market Profile

Shows **how volume is distributed by price level**, not just over time. It reveals where the market spent the most time — and therefore, where big players built their positions. The key concept here is the **Point of Control (POC)**: the price level with the highest traded volume — the "magnet" around which price tends to oscillate.

📊 How the SwipeUP Elite FX Method Uses Volume

The method combines three layers of volume data:

1. **Total Volume (Activity)**

- Measures strength of the current move.
- Rising volume + strong trend = institutional support.
- Falling volume + trend = likely exhaustion.

1. **Cluster Volume (Footprints)**

- Shows exactly *where* orders are concentrated.
- Helps locate institutional accumulation/distribution zones.

1. **Volume Profile (POC, VAH, VAL)**

- POC = Point of Control → balance level
- VAH = Value Area High → where selling begins
- VAL = Value Area Low → where buying begins

These three create a "volume map"
showing whether institutions are defending or abandoning a level.

🧠 How Institutions Use Volume

Institutions don't care about exact prices.
They care about **liquidity zones** —
areas where they can fill massive orders without moving price too fast.

When volume spikes suddenly after a long low-volume period, it means big money just stepped in.
They might even push price *against* their final direction to create the liquidity they need —
this is the classic "stop hunt."

> 🧠 Volume is the language of the invisible.
> Every spike tells you where the giants have spoken.

⚙️ How to Read Volume and Market Profile Step by Step

1. **Mark the High-Volume Nodes (HVN).**
2. These are areas of heavy trading activity —
3. potential accumulation or distribution zones.
4. **Identify the Low-Volume Nodes (LVN).**
5. These are "gaps" where price moved quickly —
6. likely to be retested later.
7. **Locate the Point of Control (POC).**
8. Price often returns here to rebalance liquidity.
9. **Watch for Volume Divergence.**
10. If price makes a new high but volume drops,
11. the move is weak — potential reversal.
12. **Confirm with Price Action (Step 2).**
13. Look for candles that align with volume expansion or rejection.

📈 Example

On **USD/JPY**,
you notice that as price rises,
volume also increases — confirming real institutional inter-

est.

But near 151.00,
volume spikes massively,
then price forms a long upper wick and reverses.
Result → high probability of institutional selling (distribution).
SwipeUP marks this zone as **institutional resistance**
and waits for confirmation of a short trade on the retest.

⚠️ Common Mistakes

1. **Ignoring volume completely.**
2. Trading without volume is like driving blind.
3. **Assuming high volume always means continuation.**
4. Sometimes it signals reversal — exhaustion or absorption.
5. **Looking at volume only on one timeframe.**
6. Always confirm across D1, H8, and H1.
7. **Forgetting the context.**
8. Volume has meaning only when compared to previous sessions.

💪 What This Step Teaches You

Once you understand volume and market profile,
you'll stop guessing where the institutions are.
You'll **see** them.
You'll know when they're building positions,
when they're taking profits,
and when they're preparing for the next move.

📊 Price tells you the story.
Volume tells you who wrote it.

Connection with the Other Steps

- **Step 6** revealed the rhythm of the market.
- **Step 7** shows *who's playing the rhythm.*
- The next step will introduce **volatility** —
- how to measure the intensity of those moves
- and adapt your strategy to different market conditions.

```
"Volume is the heartbeat of the market.
 Learn to listen, and you'll know when it's alive --
 and when it's faking."
```

8

Step 8 - Volatility: Understanding the Market's Pulse From Calm Waters to Storms — Learning When to Trade and When to Wait

Every trader has experienced it:
one day the market moves like a glacier,
and the next, it explodes in every direction.
That difference is called **volatility** —
the speed and intensity of price movement.
For institutional traders, volatility is not chaos.
It's opportunity.
The **Eighth Step of the SwipeUP Elite FX Method**
teaches you how to measure and interpret volatility,
so you can adapt your strategy to the rhythm of the market
and never be caught unprepared when the storm hits.

🎯 Goal of This Step

To understand how volatility affects risk, timing, and decision-making —
and how to adjust your trades according to it.
High volatility means big opportunities *and* big danger.
Low volatility means safety *but* fewer chances.
The key is to recognize which phase you're in
and adapt like an institution would.

> 💡 Volatility is neither good nor bad.
> It's simply the market breathing.

🔍 What Is Volatility

Volatility measures **how much and how fast** price changes within a given period.
There are two main types:

1. **Historical Volatility** – how much price has moved in the past.
2. **Implied Volatility** – how much the market *expects* it to move in the future
3. (based on options and institutional pricing).

In practical terms:

- High volatility = wide candles, strong moves, emotional traders.
- Low volatility = small candles, sideways movement, waiting periods.

📊 How SwipeUP Elite FX Measures Volatility

The method uses a combination of technical and statistical tools to define the volatility regime in real time:

1. Average True Range (ATR)

Shows the average range of price movement.

- Rising ATR → expanding volatility (prepare for bigger swings).
- Falling ATR → contracting volatility (range or consolidation).

2. Bollinger Bands

Visualize volatility boundaries.

- When bands widen → volatility surge.
- When bands contract → volatility squeeze (often before big breakouts).

3. Session Volatility Index

Measures typical volatility by market session:

- London = most active
- New York = highly reactive
- Asia = slow and steady

SwipeUP uses this to identify **"killer hours"** —

moments when volatility becomes too chaotic to manage safely.

🧠 How Institutions Use Volatility

Institutions love volatility — but only when *they* control it.
They increase volatility to trigger retail stop losses and collect liquidity.
Then they reduce volatility to trap traders in boredom and accumulate positions quietly.
When volatility suddenly expands after a long calm period, it's often **the start of a new institutional move**.

> 🧠 Institutions create volatility to make retail traders emotional.
> The calm before the move is never an accident.

⚙️ How to Trade with Volatility

1. **Identify the current regime.**
2. Use ATR or Bollinger Bands to see if volatility is high or low.
3. **Adapt your position size.**

- High volatility → smaller position.
- Low volatility → larger position possible.

1. **Adjust Stop Loss and Take Profit.**

- SL should be at least 1× ATR.
- TP should reflect volatility expansion potential (2× ATR or

more).

1. **Avoid "Killer Hours."**
2. Don't open trades during overlapping sessions
3. (e.g., London + New York) unless confirmed by institutional volume.
4. **Use volatility compression as a setup.**
5. A long period of low volatility often precedes a breakout.
6. The smaller the range, the stronger the coming move.

📈 Example

On **EUR/USD**,
ATR drops for three days — volatility contraction.
Bollinger Bands narrow tightly around price.
Then, during London's opening,
a strong breakout occurs with expanding volume —
volatility suddenly spikes.
SwipeUP recognizes this as a **volatility breakout**,
confirming entry with Price Action and momentum alignment.
The trade reaches Take Profit within hours.

⚠️ Common Mistakes

1. **Ignoring volatility altogether.**
2. Using the same Stop Loss size every time is a recipe for disaster.
3. **Trading during news events blindly.**
4. Volatility during news can invalidate any technical setup.
5. **Confusing fast moves with high volatility.**

6. A big candle without follow-through is just a liquidity spike.
7. **Overreacting to noise.**
8. Volatility is natural — don't let it push you into emotional trading.

🧠 What This Step Teaches You

Once you master volatility,
you'll stop fearing market speed.
You'll know when to act, when to wait,
and how to size your trades intelligently.
Volatility becomes your compass, not your enemy.

> 📊 Volatility doesn't destroy traders.
> Misunderstanding it does.

Connection with the Other Steps

- **Step 7** showed you *where* institutional activity is hidden.
- **Step 8** reveals *how powerful* that activity can become.
- The next step — Step 9 — will teach you how to use **statistics**
- to measure pattern reliability and probability of success.

```
"Don't fight volatility -- dance with it.
 The storm doesn't sink those who know how to surf
 it."
```

9

Step 9 - Statistical Patterns: Turning Probability into Precision From Guesswork to Measured Confidence

Most retail traders rely on intuition.
They "feel" that the market will rise or fall,
but feelings have no place in professional trading.

Institutions don't guess — they measure.
They analyze thousands of historical cases
to understand what's likely to happen next,
not what they hope will happen.

The Ninth Step of the SwipeUP Elite FX Method
transforms your approach from emotional to statistical,
teaching you how to assign probabilities to your trades
and choose only those that have a measurable edge.

🎯 Goal of This Step

To use statistics and data to validate every trade setup.
Instead of asking "Will this trade work?",
you'll ask:

"How often does this pattern succeed under these conditions?"

This step gives you confidence built on math — not luck.

💡 The market rewards probability, not prediction.

🔍 What Are Statistical Patterns

A statistical pattern is a recurring price behavior
that has shown a consistent outcome over time.

For example:

A bullish engulfing candle at a weekly support
might have a 65% chance of reversal.

A false breakout during high retail long positions
might succeed 70% of the time.

SwipeUP Elite FX collects and backtests these behaviors
to determine which ones are truly reliable.

📊 How the SwipeUP Elite FX Method Uses Statistics

The method evaluates each setup using four layers of probability:

Historical Probability (Backtesting)

How often the same pattern led to profit in the past.

Minimum threshold: 70% success rate across 1000+ samples.

Conditional Probability

How likely the pattern works given certain conditions (trend direction, volatility, sentiment alignment).

Statistical Expectancy

Average win × probability − average loss × probability.

Ensures that even if you lose, long-term expectancy stays positive.

Scenario Simulation

The method simulates 10 future price paths (candles, 8H).

If even one realistic scenario hits Stop Loss before Take Profit, the trade is rejected.

🧠 How Institutions Think About Probability

Institutions don't care about being right on every trade. They care about being profitable across hundreds of trades.

They think in terms of sample size:

if a setup works 8 out of 10 times,
they'll take it a hundred times —
and accept the two losses as part of the cost.

This is why emotion-free discipline matters more than intuition.

🧠 Retail traders want to be right.
Institutions want to be consistent.

⚙️ How to Build Statistical Confidence Step by Step

Record every trade setup.

Include pattern, time, volatility level, sentiment data.

Group similar setups.

Example: "Breakout + Retest with RSI confirmation."

Backtest at least 100 historical cases.

Use TradingView or Excel to log results.

Calculate win rate and average reward/risk ratio.

Win rate × Reward/Risk = statistical expectancy.

Accept only setups with long-term expectancy > 1.2.
(Means: for every $1 risked, you expect $1.20 in return over time.)

📈 Example

Suppose your "Post-Manipulation Entry" pattern
wins 73% of the time
with an average Reward/Risk ratio of 2.0.

Statistical expectancy =
$(0.73 \times 2) - (0.27 \times 1) = +1.19$

That means every dollar risked
has an average expected return of $1.19 —
a true institutional-grade edge.

⚠ Common Mistakes

Judging from small samples.
Ten trades aren't data — they're coincidence.

Ignoring losing trades.
Every failure teaches how conditions affect the setup.

Forcing probabilities to fit your bias.
The numbers don't care about your opinion.

Abandoning the method after one loss.
Even a 70% system loses three times in ten.

💪 What This Step Teaches You

After mastering statistics,
you stop trading based on emotion.

You'll treat each setup like a scientist:
hypothesis, test, result, adjustment.

Losses won't scare you —
because you'll know they're already part of the math.

📊 Confidence doesn't come from winning every trade.
It comes from knowing your numbers are on your side.

"Trading isn't about certainty. It's about having a small edge and repeating it relentlessly."

10

Step 10 - Confirmation and Confluence: Building Trades Like an Institution From Single Signals to Complete Systems

In the retail world, most traders act on one clue —

a candle pattern, a moving average cross,

or a news headline.

But in the institutional world, one signal means nothing.

Banks and hedge funds act **only when multiple independent factors align**.

That alignment is called **confluence** —

the harmony between technical, statistical, and fundamental evidence.

The **Tenth Step of the SwipeUP Elite FX Method**

teaches you how to combine signals into a structured confirmation system,

just like institutional analysts do before placing millions on a trade.

🎯 Goal of This Step

To ensure that every trade setup you take
is backed by **multiple layers of confirmation**,
each validating the others.
A single green light can mislead you.
Three or four lights pointing in the same direction?
That's a trade institutions would take.

> 💡 One clue is opinion.
> Many clues form evidence.

🔍 What Is Confluence in Trading

Confluence is when several independent analyses
point to the same conclusion.
For example:

- Price Action shows a bullish engulfing candle,
- RSI confirms momentum,
- Volume increases,
- and fundamentals support a strong currency.

Together, they create **a statistically powerful signal**
that goes beyond guesswork.
SwipeUP Elite FX defines confluence as a *minimum of three independent confirmations*
across different modules

📊 The Three Pillars of Confirmation

1. **Technical Confirmation**

- Structure, trend, and key levels from Steps 1–5.
- Breakout or retest aligned with institutional zones.

1. **Statistical Confirmation**

- Historical probability (Step 9).
- Positive expectancy proven through data.

1. **Fundamental Confirmation**

- Macro and monetary policy coherence (Steps 11–13).
- Institutional flow supports technical direction.

When these three align,
the trade becomes not just "good-looking" — it becomes **institutional-grade**.

🧠 How Institutions Think About Confluence

Institutional traders have entire teams
analyzing each layer separately:
technical desks, macro desks, quant models.
A trade only passes through if *all* departments agree.
That's why big moves rarely fail:
they're backed by data, policy, and psychology together.

🧠 Retail traders look for signals.

Institutions build consensus.

⚙️? How to Build Confluence Step by Step

1. **Start from Structure (Step 1).**
2. Confirm direction and main trend.
3. **Add Price Action (Step 2).**
4. Wait for manipulation and clear entry pattern.
5. **Check Volume and Volatility (Steps 7–8).**
6. The move must have strength, not just shape.
7. **Validate with Statistics (Step 9).**
8. Backtested pattern + positive expectancy = reliability.
9. **Confirm with Fundamentals.**
10. Ensure macro conditions don't contradict your direction.
11. **Final Filter: Sentiment.**
12. If retail traders are heavily positioned the opposite way → green light.

Only after all six layers confirm
is the trade authorized by the SwipeUP model.

📈 Example

You're analyzing **USD/CHF**:

- D1 structure: clear uptrend (Step 1).
- Price Action: post-manipulation bullish engulfing (Step 2).
- Volume: increasing (Step 7).
- ATR: volatility expansion (Step 8)
- Pattern: 74% success rate historically (Step 9).
- Fundamentals: FED hawkish, SNB dovish (Step 13).

Result → full institutional confluence.
SwipeUP flags the trade as "confirmed and ready."
That's how banks operate — and now, so do you.

⚠️ Common Mistakes

1. **Relying on one confirmation.**
2. A good candle or indicator alone means nothing.
3. **Adding too many redundant signals.**
4. Five oscillators showing the same thing = one confirmation, not five.
5. **Ignoring contradictions.**
6. If even one major module disagrees, the trade must wait.
7. **Forcing alignment.**
8. True confluence happens naturally — never twist data to fit your bias.

💪 What This Step Teaches You

Once you master confluence,
your trades become cleaner, rarer, and far more profitable.
You'll learn to ignore 90% of the noise
and focus on the few setups that institutions are likely taking too.
You'll stop being a guesser
and start thinking like a portfolio manager.

> 📊 Discipline is saying "no" to every trade
> until the evidence says "yes."

Connection with the Other Steps

- **Step 9** gave you the numbers behind your edge.
- **Step 10** teaches you how to combine that edge with confirmation.
- The next step — Step 11 — will take you into the **macroeconomic dimension**,
- where you'll understand how global data and central banks
- truly move the currencies you trade.

```
"A professional trader doesn't take more trades.
 He takes better ones -- built on evidence, not
 emotion."
```

11

Step 11 – Macroeconomic Data: Reading the Market's Heartbeat Understanding How Global Events Move Currencies

Behind every candle on your chart
lies an entire world of economic forces —
interest rates, inflation, jobs, and growth.
These numbers may look abstract,
but for institutions, they are **the heartbeat of the market**.
The **Eleventh Step of the SwipeUP Elite FX Method**
teaches you to interpret macroeconomic data like a professional analyst:
to understand *why* currencies rise or fall
and how to prepare before big economic releases move the charts.

🎯 Goal of This Step

To connect **economic events and data**
to their direct impact on currency movements,
so that you trade in harmony with institutional money flow.
Most retail traders ignore macro data or fear it.
SwipeUP traders use it as a **map** of institutional decisions.

> 💡 Price is the effect.
> Macroeconomics is the cause.

🔍 What Is Macroeconomic Data

Macroeconomic data measures the health of a country's economy.
Institutions monitor these indicators daily
to decide where to invest, lend, or withdraw capital.
Here are the **key data points** that move the Forex market most:
Indicator Meaning Impact
CPI (Consumer Price Index)
Measures inflation
High CPI → currency strengthens (expect higher interest rates)
GDP (Gross Domestic Product)
Measures growth
Strong GDP → stronger currency
Unemployment Rate
Labor market health
Lower unemployment → stronger economy
PMI (Purchasing Managers' Index)
Business activity
Above 50 = expansion, below 50 = contraction

Retail Sales
Consumer strength
Rising sales → more growth, higher inflation risk
Trade Balance
Exports minus imports
Positive = capital inflows (currency support)

🧠 How Institutions Use Macroeconomic Data

For institutional traders,
macroeconomic releases are not "news events" —
they are **capital reallocation triggers**.
When inflation rises,
banks expect central banks to raise interest rates,
so they start buying that currency weeks in advance.
When GDP contracts,
they anticipate cuts and move money elsewhere.
Every data point shifts billions of dollars.
SwipeUP traders learn to anticipate those shifts,
not to react after they happen.

> 🧠 Institutions don't trade the news.
> They trade the expectations behind the news.

⚙️ How to Read Macroeconomic Data Step by Step

1. **Check the Economic Calendar Daily.**
2. Use reliable sources like Investing.com or ForexFactory.
3. **Note the "Expected" vs. "Previous" Values.**

- If actual > expected → bullish for the currency.

- If actual < expected → bearish.

1. **Understand the Context.**
2. A single number doesn't matter — the *trend* does.
3. For example, three months of rising inflation
4. signal a lasting impact on monetary policy.
5. **Watch Market Reaction.**
6. Sometimes good data causes a drop —
7. this means the market had already *priced it in.*
8. Institutions move based on surprise, not headlines.
9. **Correlate with Policy Expectations.**
10. Rising inflation + central bank concern = rate hike potential (currency bullish).
11. Weak growth + falling inflation = rate cut potential (currency bearish).

📈 Example

Let's say the **U.S. CPI** comes out at 4.2% (expected 3.7%).

Retail traders see the spike and chase USD longs.

But SwipeUP traders were already prepared —

the previous week's PMI and wage data hinted at rising inflation.

They entered early, before the crowd.

When the CPI data is released,

institutions simply take profits as retail traders join late.

Result → You profit with the institutions, not against them.

⚠️ Common Mistakes

1. **Trading during the news release.**
2. Volatility is unpredictable in the first minutes.
3. **Ignoring the forecast.**
4. The market moves based on expectations, not the number itself.
5. **Overreacting to a single report.**
6. Always confirm trends across multiple data points.
7. **Forgetting the bigger picture.**
8. A strong GDP doesn't help if inflation is out of control.

💪 What This Step Teaches You

You'll stop fearing economic announcements
and start reading them like a professional economist.
You'll understand the logic behind every institutional move
and use that knowledge to stay ahead of the crowd.
When you combine macro data with technical analysis,
your trades gain purpose — not just precision.

> 📊 The market moves on numbers,
> but profits move to those who understand them first.

Connection with the Other Steps

- **Step 10** taught you to build multi-layered confirmation.
- **Step 11** now adds the *economic foundation* behind those confirmations.
- The next step — Step 12 — will show you how to interpret

economic surprises
- and the emotional reactions they trigger in the market.

```
"Don't trade the candle -- trade the reason it
exists."
```

12

Step 12 – Economic Surprises: When the Market Gets Caught Off Guard Learning to Trade What No One Expected

Every trader has seen it:

a news number comes out *better* than expected,
yet the market suddenly drops instead of rising.
Why does that happen?
Because institutions were already prepared —
and retail traders were not.
The **Twelfth Step of the SwipeUP Elite FX Method**
teaches you how to understand and trade **economic surprises**,
the moments when reality diverges from expectation —
and when the biggest opportunities are born.

🎯 Goal of This Step

To learn how to interpret the **difference between forecast and actual data**,
and to anticipate how institutions will react to that difference.
Markets don't move on the news itself —
they move on whether the news *surprises* or *confirms* expectations.

> 💡 The number doesn't move the market.
> The surprise behind it does.

🔍 What Is an Economic Surprise

Every major data release — CPI, GDP, jobs, PMI —
comes with three key numbers:

- **Previous** → the last reported value
- **Forecast** → what analysts expect
- **Actual** → the real number just released

The difference between "Forecast" and "Actual"
is what traders call the **economic surprise**.
The greater the surprise,
the stronger the institutional reaction.

📊 Example of Market Reaction

Let's say the **U.S. Non-Farm Payrolls (NFP)** report:

- Forecast: +150K new jobs

- Actual: +300K

That's a **positive surprise** — the U.S. economy is stronger than expected

Retail traders rush to buy USD immediately.
But institutional traders?
They had already bought USD two days earlier,
based on private labor data (ADP, unemployment claims).
When the NFP number is released,
they use the retail buying frenzy to **take profit**.
Result → USD falls even after a "good" number.
It wasn't manipulation — it was preparation.

> 🧠 Institutions react to expectations,
> not to headlines.

⚙️ How to Analyze Economic Surprises Step by Step

1. **Compare Forecast vs Actual.**

- If Actual > Forecast → positive surprise (bullish potential).
- If Actual < Forecast → negative surprise (bearish potential).

1. **Check Market Reaction in the First Minutes.**

- Is the reaction aligned with the data or the opposite?
- A move *against* the data = profit-taking or trap.

1. **Evaluate Previous Market Positioning.**

- If the market was already long,

- even good data can trigger a selloff.

1. **Observe Volatility.**

- Strong spikes + immediate reversal = retail liquidation.
- Controlled move with follow-through = institutional continuation.

1. **Confirm with Volume and Sentiment.**

- High volume + contrarian sentiment = institutional dominance.

📈 Example

EUR/USD before ECB interest rate decision:

- Forecast: no rate change (4.50%)
- Actual: rate hike to 4.75% → positive surprise for EUR.

Price spikes upward immediately —
but within 30 minutes, it collapses lower.
Why?
Because institutions had already positioned long EUR
before the meeting.
When the surprise confirmed their bias,
they exited to lock profits.
Retail traders who entered late lost money.

⚠️ Common Mistakes

1. **Trading the news instantly.**
2. Institutional algorithms react in milliseconds — you can't beat them.
3. **Ignoring the forecast.**
4. Without knowing the expected value,
5. you can't measure the surprise.
6. **Assuming the first move is real.**
7. Often it's just stop hunting and liquidity collection.
8. **Overtrading news events.**
9. High volatility doesn't mean high opportunity.

💪 What This Step Teaches You

You'll stop chasing headlines
and start *reading between the numbers.*
You'll know when a "good" report is already priced in
and when a surprise really changes the game.
You'll wait for the emotion to fade
and trade the logical direction —
the one institutions quietly follow after the noise.

> 📊 Markets don't move on information.
> They move on disappointment and surprise.

Connection with the Other Steps

- **Step 11** taught you how to understand macroeconomic data. **Step 12** now reveals how to interpret *the difference*
- between data and expectation — the true trigger for volatil-

ity.

- The next step — **Step 13** — will take you inside
- the decision-making of **central banks**,
- showing how monetary policy transforms data into real price movement.

```
"Don't react to the news.
 React to how the market reacts to the news."
```

13

Step 13 – Monetary Policy: The Central Banks' Master Plan Understanding Who Truly Moves the Market

If the Forex market were a chessboard,
central banks would be the grandmasters moving all the pieces.
They decide how much money circulates,
how expensive it is to borrow,
and which economies will grow or slow down.
Every other player — from hedge funds to retail traders —
simply reacts to their moves.
The **Thirteenth Step of the SwipeUP Elite FX Method**
teaches you to think like a central banker:
to anticipate the logic behind interest rate changes,
and to understand how those decisions
shape every currency on your chart.

🎯 Goal of This Step

To learn how **monetary policy** controls currency value,
and how to align your trades
with the long-term direction dictated by central banks.
When you know what the policymakers are aiming for,
you can position yourself *before* the big moves happen.

> 💡 You don't fight the banks.
> You follow their flow.

🔍 What Is Monetary Policy

Monetary policy is the process through which central banks
manage money supply and interest rates
to maintain economic stability.
It determines:

- how expensive it is to borrow money,
- how much credit flows through the economy, and
- ultimately, how strong a currency becomes.

There are two key phases of policy:

1. **Tightening (Hawkish)** → higher interest rates → stronger currency.
2. **Easing (Dovish)** → lower interest rates → weaker currency.

📊 Main Policy Tools Used by Central Banks

Tool Description Market Effect

Interest Rate Decisions

Main instrument to control inflation

Higher rates = stronger currency

Quantitative Easing (QE)

Buying assets to inject money

Weakens currency

Quantitative Tightening (QT)

Selling assets to remove liquidity

Strengthens currency

Forward Guidance

Future policy communication

Shapes expectations before action

Balance Sheet Control

Adjusting asset holdings

Influences long-term capital flows

Every announcement, speech, or document from a central bank contains clues about future moves.

SwipeUP traders learn to read those clues before they become headlines.

🧠 How Institutions Trade Around Monetary Policy

Institutions don't wait for policy meetings.

They position themselves weeks in advance, based on inflation data, employment trends, and central bank tone.

When a bank becomes *hawkish* (concerned about inflation), they buy that currency.

When it turns *dovish* (worried about growth), they sell it.
Retail traders usually react after the decision — institutions profit because they've anticipated it.

> 🧠 Central banks move policy slowly.
> Institutions move before everyone else.

⚙️ How to Read Central Bank Behavior Step by Step

1. **Follow Official Communications.**

- Press conferences, meeting minutes, and public speeches.
- Watch the tone: *hawkish* = strong, *dovish* = weak.

1. **Track Inflation and Growth Data.**

- Rising inflation pushes banks toward rate hikes.
- Slowing growth forces them to ease.

1. **Compare Two Currencies.**
2. Forex is always relative.

- If FED is hawkish and ECB is dovish → USD strengthens vs EUR.

1. **Anticipate Market Pricing.**

- Futures and swaps (CME FedWatch) show what the market expects.
- If expectations shift, currencies move immediately.

1. **Confirm with Institutional Volume.**

- Volume surges before rate decisions often reveal early positioning.

📈 Example

Suppose the **Federal Reserve (FED)** signals
that inflation is still too high and "further hikes may be needed."
That tone is *hawkish*.
SwipeUP reads this as USD bullish pressure.
If at the same time, the **European Central Bank (ECB)**
says it will "pause rate increases,"
then EUR weakens.
Result → EUR/USD short setup,
confirmed by fundamentals and volume alignment.

⚠️ Common Mistakes

1. **Ignoring central bank tone.**
2. A single phrase can move billions.
3. **Reacting only to decisions, not to guidance.**
4. The real move happens when policy direction changes, not rates themselves.
5. **Forgetting the relative nature of Forex.**
6. A strong USD doesn't matter if EUR is even stronger.
7. **Trading too close to policy announcements.**
8. High volatility can distort normal setups.

💪 What This Step Teaches You

Once you understand monetary policy,
you'll stop fearing rate decisions —
you'll start predicting them.
You'll know when a central bank is preparing a major shift,
and you'll align your trades with those who control liquidity.
You'll trade with the current, not against it.

📊 The charts show the result.
Central banks write the script.

Connection with the Other Steps

- **Step 12** taught you how to interpret economic surprises.
- **Step 13** explains the logic behind them — the response mechanism of central banks.
- The next step — **Step 14** — will show you how to compare these monetary policies
- between currencies, revealing which one truly leads the market.

```
"When the central banks speak,
 the market doesn't listen -- it obeys."
```

14

Step 14 - Relative Strength Between Currencies: Finding the True Market Leader Discovering Which Currency Drives and Which One Follows

Every Forex pair is a tug-of-war between two currencies.
When EUR/USD rises, is it because the euro is strong —
or because the dollar is weak?
Understanding the answer to that question
is the secret behind institutional-level trading.
The **Fourteenth Step of the SwipeUP Elite FX Method**
teaches you how to measure and compare the strength of currencies,
to identify which one truly commands the market —
and which one is simply reacting.

🎯 Goal of This Step

To learn how to calculate and interpret **relative strength** between two currencies,
so you can trade in the direction of the dominant force.
You'll stop guessing which way the market "feels" like going,
and start *quantifying* which currency is in control.

> 💡 Price moves when one side wins the strength battle.

🔍 What Is Relative Strength

Relative strength compares how strong or weak each individual currency is across all major pairs.
For example:
If EUR is gaining against USD, GBP, and CHF,
while USD is falling against most others,
then EUR is strong and USD is weak.
The stronger currency pulls the weaker one,
and their combination defines the trend direction.
SwipeUP uses this logic to filter trades:
we always want to **buy the strong** and **sell the weak**.

📊 How SwipeUP Measures Relative Strength

The method combines technical, macro, and sentiment data to calculate a **dynamic strength score (0–100)** for each currency.

1. Technical Component

- Direction of D1 and H8 trends.
- Position relative to 200-period MA.
- Momentum (RSI / WaveTrend alignment).

2. Fundamental Component

- Monetary policy tone (Step 13).
- Inflation, GDP, and employment data (Steps 11–12).

3. Sentiment and Positioning

- Retail trader exposure (from MyFxBook, FXSSI).
- Option and futures data (CME, FXBlue).

All scores are normalized and averaged.
The difference between two currencies' scores creates the **Relative Strength Differential (RSD)**.

📈 Example

Currency Strength Score
EUR
76
USD
48
JPY
42
GBP
66

CHF
52
In this case, **EUR** is the strongest, **JPY** the weakest.
SwipeUP would look for **EUR/JPY long** setups,
or **JPY/USD short**, depending on structure alignment.
If EUR = 76 and USD = 48,
the **RSD = +28**, signaling a clear bullish bias for EUR/USD.

🧠 How Institutions Use Relative Strength

Institutions don't trade "pairs."
They trade **flows** —
allocations of capital between currencies based on strength shifts.
When central banks change tone or macro data shifts,
funds rotate money from weak to strong economies.
For example:
if the ECB turns hawkish while the FED stays neutral,
capital flows from USD assets into EUR assets.
That's why EUR/USD rises.
Retail traders see candles.
Institutions see **global money movement**.

> 🧠 Every candle on your chart
> is a symptom of capital migration.

⚙️ How to Use Relative Strength Step by Step

1. **Update Currency Strength Table Daily.**
2. Use D1 data to see which currencies are gaining or losing momentum.

3. **Identify the Top 2 and Bottom 2.**
4. The strongest and weakest currencies create your best opportunities.
5. **Check Multi-Timeframe Alignment.**
6. H8 and H1 must confirm the same direction as D1.
7. **Confirm with Volume and Policy.**
8. Ensure institutional volume supports the direction,
9. and that monetary policies between the two currencies diverge.
10. **Enter Only When Differential > 20 Points.**
11. Anything smaller means equilibrium — no clear flow yet.

📈 Practical Example

- EUR strength = 80 (hawkish ECB).
- CAD strength = 53 (neutral BoC, weaker oil).
- RSD = +27 → **EUR/CAD long** bias.

If technical structure (Step 1) and Price Action (Step 2)
confirm the same bullish pattern,
SwipeUP authorizes the trade as *institutional grade*.

⚠️ Common Mistakes

1. **Judging by one pair only.**
2. Strength must be measured across the market, not in isolation.
3. **Ignoring policy divergence.**
4. Strong fundamentals beat short-term chart noise.
5. **Using outdated data.**
6. Strength changes daily — update scores regularly.

7. **Trading equilibrium zones.**
8. If both currencies are equally strong or weak, price stagnates.

💪 What This Step Teaches You

Once you master relative strength,
you'll always know *who's really in control* of every move.
You'll stop fighting the flow and start surfing it.
You'll learn to follow institutional capital
as it migrates from weak economies to strong ones —
the real engine behind every Forex trend.

> 📊 Trade strength against weakness.
> That's the only rule the banks respect.

Connection with the Other Steps

- **Step 13** taught you how central banks shape strength.
- **Step 14** quantifies it across all currencies.
- The next step — **Step 15** — will reveal
- how institutional flows (COT data and order positioning)
- confirm these strength shifts in real time.

```
"Don't just follow the price --
 follow the power behind it."
```

15

Conclusion

Conclusion - You Are the Method

The journey you've just completed isn't just a trading manual.

It's a transformation in how you see the market — and yourself.

You started this book maybe out of curiosity,
or because you wanted to understand
why most traders lose while only a few truly win.
Now you know the truth:
those who win don't *follow* the price — they *anticipate* it.
Those who lose, react instead of plan.
The **SwipeUP Elite FX Method** was never meant
to give you signals or shortcuts.
It was built to shape your mind
into that of an institutional trader —
logical, patient, data-driven, and emotionally resilient.

Each of the 35 steps has guided you through that transformation:

from confusion to structure,
from instinct to discipline,
from randomness to precision.
You've learned that discipline beats luck,
that patience is stronger than excitement,
and that consistency matters more than perfection.

The New You

From this point on,
you're not just a trader — you're an observer,
a strategist who understands the forces behind every move.
You'll no longer be fooled by random spikes or fake rallies.
You'll see the truth beneath the candles —
the psychology of thc crowd,
the logic of institutions,
and the rhythm that drives every market.
You now speak **the hidden language of price**.
And like any language,
the more you use it, the more fluent you'll become.

The Real Victory

The real victory isn't one winning trade —
it's mastering yourself.
It's the ability to stay calm when everyone panics.
To follow your plan even when emotions scream otherwise.
To protect your capital when the crowd burns theirs.
Because the market doesn't reward who guesses right.
It rewards who stays consistent —
day after day, trade after trade.

🧠 "I execute the plan, I don't suffer it.
I trade like institutions — against the retail crowd.
Discipline and patience above all."

The Legacy of SwipeUP Elite FX

There is no secret formula.
No shortcut.
Only data, logic, and emotional control.
And when you combine those three,
you'll never need luck again.
You'll be the trader others try to understand —
the one who seems to "always be on the right side."
Because now you don't just trade the market.
You understand it.
And understanding lasts forever.

📄 The market never really changes.
What changes is how clearly you see it.

```
"Don't try to predict the future.
 Learn to recognize when it's already written."-
  Andrea Russo, creator of the SwipeUP Elite FX Method
```

Afterword

"If after reading all this you still think Forex is a matter of luck...
then close the book, scratch off a ticket, and let me know if you win—
so we can at least backtest that!"

About the Author

My name is Andrea Russo, and for over ten years I've been immersed in the world of Forex.

Not as a spectator, but as an independent institutional trader,
who grew up observing how banks,
funds, hedge funds, and above all, how losing traders think, really move.

I started like many others: with enthusiasm, curiosity, and a fair share of mistakes.

Over time, I've understood that the market isn't a place of chance,
but a complex language that only a few truly learn to decipher.
And that the difference between winners and losers
is not in the chart, but in the mind.

In ten years of experience,
I've seen hundreds of strategies fail and few survive.
I've managed capital,
not to prove something,

but to build a method that could last over time,
a system capable of filtering out the noise and bringing out only what matters.

From all this, the SwipeUP Elite FX Method was born:
a synthesis of years of study, testing, mistakes, and victories,
designed for those who finally want to understand
how those who really move the market think.

You won't find magic formulas or secrets from course salesmen in these pages.
Instead, you'll find a method—logical, rigorous, and human—
that will teach you to look at Forex with completely different eyes.

I'm writing this book not to show you how much I know, but to share what I wish I'd known at the beginning: how to avoid traps, how to recognize strong hands, and how to become a trader who doesn't follow the crowd, but rather anticipates it.

This isn't a technical manual: it's a journey into the institutional mind, written for those who have decided to stop guessing and start understanding.

Welcome to the SwipeUP Elite FX Method. Your true journey as a professional begins here.

You can connect with me on:

https://andrearussoforextrader.com

Printed in Poland
by Amazon Fulfillment
Poland Sp. z o.o., Wrocław

62741357R00060